HOODWINKED

Poems

———

DAVID HERNANDEZ

———————

Winner of the 2010 Kathryn A. Morton Prize in Poetry
Selected by Amy Gerstler

Sarabande S Books
LOUISVILLE, KENTUCKY

Managing Editor
Sarabande Books, Inc.
2234 Dundee Road, Suite 200
Louisville, KY 40205

Library of Congress Cataloging-in-Publication Data

Hernandez, David, 1971–
 Hoodwinked : poems / by David Hernandez. — 1st ed.
   p. cm.
 "Winner of the 2010 Kathryn A. Morton Prize in Poetry, selected by Amy Gerstler."
 ISBN 978-1-932511-96-3 (pbk. : alk. paper)
 I. Title.
 PS3608.E766H66 2011
 811'.6—dc22
                      2010050714
 ISBN-13: 978-1-932511-96-3

Cover Image: "Origami, 2005" by Kumi Yamashita. Light, aluminum, shadow. Photograph provided courtesy of the artist.
Cover and text design by Kirkby Gann Tittle.

Manufactured in Canada.
This book is printed on acid-free paper.

Sarabande Books is a nonprofit literary organization.

 The Kentucky Arts Council, the state arts agency, supports Sarabande Books with state tax dollars and federal funding from the National Endowment for the Arts.

for Lisa

CONTENTS

ACKNOWLEDGMENTS

Thank you to the editors of the following magazines where these poems first appeared:

AGNI Online   "Everything I'm About to Tell You Actually Happened," "Flipbook," "Supermarkets This Large"

Bat City Review   "Snowman"

The Cincinnati Review   "Head Case," "Victory Song"

diode   "Closer," "Hangover," "Self-Portrait with Baby Possum"

FIELD   "American Water," "Fooling the Buffalo," "Moose in Snow," "Panoramic"

5 AM   "The Body You're Suited-up In"

Gargoyle   "The Pompous Man"

Gulf Coast   "The Big Nothing, or the Gap Between David Letterman's Teeth," "Proof," "Why Maggots"

Ghost Town   "Obituary"

Harvard Review   "On Aggression"

Hayden's Ferry Review   "Phantom Limb"

Indiana Review   "Fear and Logic"

The Kenyon Review   "Mosul"

Konundrum Engine Literary Review   "Trompe L'Oeil"

The Missouri Review   "Retirement Home Melee at the Salad Bar"

Narrative   "At the Post Office," "Kindergarten," "Questions About Butterflies," "Velvet"

Prairie Schooner   "Married And," "Road Trip"

Rattle   "Remember It Wrong"

Shade   "Man with Swatter"

32 Poems   "Housefly"

"On Aggression" also appeared on *Poetry Daily*.

"Married And" and "Road Trip" received the Glenna Luschei *Prairie Schooner* Award in 2008.

My heartfelt appreciation goes out to Jim McMichael and Michael Ryan for their infinite wisdom; to Sarah Gorham, Jeffrey Skinner, and all the wonderful people at Sarabande; to Amy Gerstler for believing in the book; to my family for their love and encouragement; and to my wife Lisa Glatt for her insights, guidance, patience, good humor, and bottomless love.

DAVID HERNANDEZ: EYES WIDE OPEN

"Hoodwinked" is a feisty, evocative word, with a whiff of mischief about it. As employed by David Hernandez in titling his third poetry collection, the term serves as a wake up call, at once goofy protest (we've been had!) and quiet warning to stay engaged every waking minute—*Don't let the wool be pulled over your eyes. Don't avert your gaze from events taking place on life's main stages, or in its smaller theaters of operation,* these poems remind us. *And don't blind yourself to the scuttling of Earth's most infinitesimal citizens, those in the insect kingdom. Pay scrupulous attention to everything till you have no more consciousness left, till you too are at last dismantled crumb by crumb by the ultimate recyclers, those industrious bugs.* ("So too the departed are taken apart and ferried elsewhere." ["Hornet's Nest."])

For me, this book has a unified, inclusive, individual voice. And although *Hoodwinked*'s title definitely suggests forms of foolery (some amusing, others malevolent or threatening) the speaker in these poems is never a dupe. On the contrary, this collection's personable protagonist is wide-awake, self-implicating, undeceived, blunt, unpretentious, and acutely observant, often veering into humor or surrealism, but using these modes judiciously. Somehow this speaker, via his focus and restraint, manages beauty of utterance and flights of dreaminess without ever straying far from the bedrock of the here and now, or his deeper themes.

No less potent for their apparent modesty of site, occasion or viewpoint, these poems often take place close to home: in a barbershop or clinic, in line at the post office, at the supermarket, in a neighbor's yard, at a less-than-idyllic family Christmas gathering, or in the mind of a man perched atop a ladder while trying to plug a hole under his roof, in an attempt to stop possum traffic into his attic. The speaker in this book offers us nothing less than a poetry of quotidian witness, embracing what Charles Simic (a poet Hernandez admires) often insists in print, "A 'truth' detached and purified of pleasures of ordinary life is not worth a damn in my view." I would even go so far as to say that the single columns or couplets Hernandez favors as poetic forms seem further evidence of his saluting the concrete and the everyday. I saw these straightforward, uncomplicated forms as analogous to basic support structures of carpentry, the vertical planks (columns) and horizontal floorboards (couplets) from which many dwellings are made.

"Hoodwinked" is a bit of lingo that finds itself saddled with sad baggage these days. The current national obsession with terrorism has made "hood" as word and image fear-producing and hopelessly loaded, bringing to mind news footage of hooded, gun-wielding perpetrators of mayhem and their helpless, hooded victims. Thus Hernandez's title is resonant with the current historical moment, and he doesn't shy away from his title's dark echoes. Though political poems don't dominate this collection, there are a handful here. Each evokes a specific situation and they often creep up on their topics indirectly. These political poems are very affecting, and wonderfully non-histrionic. In a recent e-mail, Hernandez wrote, "Although I'm still interested in mining my life for material and writing poems in the confessional vein, I'm also concerned with larger issues happening in the world and writing about them. Injustices and other crimes. Of course, I don't want these poems to sound like political commentary. How do you say 'Fuck You' to Cheney and cronies like him, but with grace and beauty? I'm still figuring out ways to do just that." I'd say he's got that covered. The poems in this collection that call attention to political violence have a deep silence in them, a quiet gravity, seeking not to rabble-rouse but to describe ever more accurately, and to create moral intimacy.

Ultimately, the lyrics in *Hoodwinked* read as odes to mortality. They marvel nonstop, unsentimentally, and with necessary ambivalence, at the world as given and the human inability to consistently rise to the exhausting challenge of making every second count. These poems constantly acknowledge that "all flesh is grass." They make us hear the wondrous, terrifying hum of impending obliteration, while at the same time never growing immune to beauty, never ceasing to be curious about what the grass itself makes of our common temporal conundrum, as in these concluding stanzas from "The Body You're Suited-up In":

There were days
when *seize the day* worked, when uttering

the phrase was an epiphany mint
sweetening your tongue. Now you might
as well be saying *seize the hammock.*

And the skull you keep on a cluttered desk
wearing a toupee of dust, how it functions
more as a paperweight than a reminder

the body you're suited-up in is a body
death is slowly unzipping. What you need
is another slogan, another *memento mori*

to replace that skull. May I suggest
an X-ray of your chest, Scotch-taped
to the kitchen window, that every morning

you study closely your heart, caught
like a child's balloon in the branches of its ribs.
Ghost-pale, as if turning to dust. Which it will.

The strength and loveliness of the images here, and the way they seamlessly transition into one another is impressive. Death slowly unzips the body while medical science bloodlessly opens the chest to reveal a ghost photo of the living heart, which mutates into a lost, deflating balloon snagged in the ribs' tree branches. There is a lightness of touch here, a sadness that rises like helium, an honoring of the ephemeral, and a grace note of wit (the "May I suggest . . ." as though a waiter is recommending a white wine to accompany today's poached Dover sole) in the face of doom that is most admirable in these poems. Congratulations, David.

—June 2010,
Amy Gerstler

1

Questions About Butterflies

We are three in a gallery high-ceilinged
and boxed in light, six eyes lost in the geometry
of butterflies jigsawed to canvas, not painted
but the actual fluttering things. Think
the shattered neon of church windows, mosaics
and kaleidoscopes. Think beauty blown apart
and pieced back together. We are six hands
flitting up to point out the multitude of wings:
yellow, owl-eyed, iridescent blue wings
and wings of velvet black, veined in green.
We are three tongues cocooned in our mouths.
I have so many questions. They had to be bred,
then exterminated. How and how? And how
many butterflies, how many days, hours
of held breath, of tweezers lifting wings?
Do butterflies suffer, does the furred
abdomen ever ache, thorax ever throb?
All those butterflies I impaled on a cactus
when I was a boy—will I go to hell for that?
Is there a heaven for butterflies and if so
how tiny the halos? Is there a God butterfly?
A Nietzsche butterfly? How many questions
about butterflies have been printed on the wings
of books? Is *Do butterflies have walking dreams?*
one of them? We are six ears and footsteps
echoing inside the gallery, then not echoing
now that we're outside, now pavement
and wind and the flight of leaves over sidewalk.
There's traffic on the drive home, the weaving

of cars and conversation. Our anxieties
and pills. Our family. Our dying, our dead.
The freeway is metal and glass going eighty,
blood orange taillights chasing blood orange
taillights. Think turn signals. Think migration.
Think of us, wingless, flying into our lives.

Fooling the Buffalo

A buffalo could outrun a lion, could outlast
a horse. Take a bullet in his shaggy head,
a buffalo could, and still roam the prairie.
Make the world rumble with his brothers,
jump as one jumped over a low wall
to escape the auction. Down an alley
and headbutt open a door, this buffalo could,
and stand majestic in a dressing room,
to gaze at the buffalo gazing at the buffalo
standing before a mirror. Could grunt,
could adore his reflection, this mammoth
beast, coffee-brown and goateed.
Indians would hunt for buffalo with a bow,
the strings made from the muscle of buffalo.
Or they hurried a herd toward a cliff,
a wooly waterfall that tumbled and bellowed.
Or ice, they coaxed the animal toward ice
to skid and stumble, easy target that bristled
with arrows. Duped toward death, the buffalo
bled on the valley floor, across the frozen
lake. Fooled toward love, the buffalo
licked the mirror, haloed in lights.
Could snort, could low, and be buffaloed.

Trompe L'Oeil

What's left of his silver hair he wants
cut so his wife would stop calling him
Mr. Cumulus. He tells his hairstylist
how short with a forefinger and thumb
centimeters apart as if showing her
an invisible pill, one of the dozen he takes
daily to keep the channels of his heart
unclogged, the blood thin, joints
without fire, the great icebergs of ache
from colliding into his body.
She turns for her scissors and turns
again to see his head shuddering
like a dandelion in an earthquake,
the cape Velcroed to his neck going up
down up down above his crotch.
She's thinking what you're thinking.
He's thinking, *I should clean my glasses*
with a handkerchief instead.
In the mirror he squints at her reflection,
pink cloud of face, orange haze
of flowerpot she raises like a trophy
before shattering it against his head.
True story, unless the hairstylist
who told the hairstylist who told
the hairstylist who's now clipping my hair
lied. Or the hairstylist twice removed
loves embellishment. This is how
every story telephoned from person
to person becomes after each telling

distorted, the way these parallel
barbershop mirrors repeat themselves
to make an endless green tunnel
I can see myself walking through.

Moose in Snow

A moose is born, his legs
unfold and wobble
beneath the weight of himself.
He grows, roams the fields, his antlers
sprout into empty hands.
Then the sky drops
snow, a meadow
fills with whiteness
the moose trudges through,
his breath in the Montana air
cobwebbing. A man
raises his camera
and the moose materializes
in the blood light of his darkroom.
A painter finds the photo
and squeezes out
titanium white, burnt umber,
works the brushes until
he has the snow-stippled coat
just right, and the visible eye
looks like the night
standing behind a peephole.
There are reproductions, rollers
spin in a print shop
and its moose moose moose
descending on itself. One man
buys one, hangs it
with a frame in his sunny office
where his patients come

troubled, medicated, and I
explain to him this heaviness
pulling down the length
of my body, scalp
to soles, cells and all.

D.F.W.

My first thought in the morning was duct tape.
Before breakfast and shower, during
breakfast and shower, and later
as I hefted into my shopping cart
a bottle of detergent: duct tape then,
the silver sheen of it, but also the noose
he looped with a black leather belt,
his head going where his stomach told him
he's hungry. My trying to forget
the details only made them more lucid,
the way the wooden patio chair
kicked over beside his feet returned to me
upright, peach-colored cedar,
lines in the grain like muscle tissue.
It's been this way since reading
the paper that ran a photo of him
unshaven and forlorn, a paisley white do-rag
wrapped so tightly around his head
it looked as if someone took a scalpel
and exposed his skull. Because he knew
his hands would stop him, he wound
his wrists together with duct tape.
How he did this confounds me still
and why sometimes I hear it
shrieking off the roller.

Remember It Wrong

> "Everyone's memory is subjective. If in three
> weeks we were both interviewed about what
> went on here tonight, we would both probably
> have very, very different stories."
> —James Frey on *Larry King Live*

> "My front four teeth are gone, I have a hole in
> my cheek, my nose is broken and my eyes are
> swollen nearly shut."
> —James Frey, from *A Million Little Pieces*

But I was there, 12C, window seat, and there
was no blood anywhere except the blue kind
making blue roots under the skin of our wrists.
From what I recall his teeth were all present,
ivory and symmetrical, one pristine incisor
flushed against the next like marble tiles.
Teeth other teeth aspire to be. I saw no hole
in his cheek but a razor nick or new pimple,
some red blip on his otherwise unblemished face.
Boyish. Babyish, even. The only holes
were the two he breathed from and the one
called a mouth that demanded another pillow,
headphones, club soda, more ice.
His nose was intact, straight as the tailfin
dividing the sky behind us. There was turbulence,
the plane a dragonfly in a windstorm.
My cup of Cabernet sloshed, my napkin bled,
a bag rumbled in the overhead bin like a fist
pounding inside a coffin. I was calm, I fly
all the time, but the man in question
was quivering and paler than a hardboiled egg.
Eyes swollen open, eyes skittering and green.

11

Or brown or blue. Memory is a murky thing,
always changing its mind. Interview me again
in three weeks and maybe I'll remember
his wounds, the way my grandmother
gradually put down the knife after she spread
butter on her napkin. Slowly the disease worked,
slowly erasing slowly what her brain slowly
recorded over the slowly decades. Memory
is a mysterious thing, shadow of a ghost,
nebulous as the clouds we pierced on our descent,
Chicago revealing itself in my little window
like dust blown from a photo of someone
it takes you a moment to recognize.

Proof

Once he wrestled a bear he said,
in a bar off-campus with eyes
glossy from lager he wrestled a bear.
Claws and all, black fur
and the salmon of his muscles
leaping under the black fur.
Wrestled and won he said,
the bear pinned and snorting,
pinned and one hundred pounds
heavier, with claws, with claws
and teeth, the electric blue current
of animal instinct. I was gullible
once, under kindergarten lights
with glitter and paste, building
a galaxy. A boy stole my stars
once, a bigger boy I wrestled
under the night of blackboard.
Wrestled and lost, pinned
and weeping with my back
to the carpet, with the fireflies
of glitter dazzling on my skin.
To the man who said he wrestled
a bear, wrestled and won,
I said, *You're full of bear shit.*
But a scar is proof and so began
the slow striptease of a pant leg
rolled to his knee. *There*, he said.
And his story sparkled on his flesh.

Why Maggots

Because the plump bags of trash slumped
beside the house like black pumpkins.
Because eleven days passed and the bags
were still there, sun-baked, fly-mobbed.
Because they sighed as I dragged them
down the driveway. Because one was torn
by a crooked nail jutting from the fence.
Because the bag grew a mouth and yawned.

So dozens tumbled onto the concrete,
minute and white. So I thought, *Rice.*
So they wriggled over the pavement
and I thought, *Not rice.* So the knotted bag
of repulsion opened in my stomach.
So I uncoiled the green hose and made
a river with my thumb, made the water
push each one under the wooden gate

and into the flowerbeds. Where they writhed.
Where in the muddy earth their spongy
and pale bodies writhed. Where marigolds
nodded yes to every come-and-go wind.
Where brown-winged butterflies mingled
and ladybugs spotted yellow petals
like flicked paint. Where nature pulled
long satin gloves over her many warts.

Flipbook

Your thumb's the projector. It's the motor
and mirror, lamp and lens. Down

the drawn frames it slides, pages purring.
Between the parted curtains of your hands

the silent movie plays out: stickman lifts
his stickarms, stickgun fires its stickbullet.

O, it's always a snuff film, always a slaying
in pencil, the way this silver man collapses,

knees bending like paperclips. Round head
to the ground, body stretched to a line,

it's easy to mistake him now for a lollipop.
The final page flips, again the first page

sits at the top, and you return to whatever it is
you do, the day calendar on your desk

shedding its days, the horizon juggling
the sun and moon, back and forth, the sun

and moon. How quickly the seven leaves
of the week fall to the earth. How boney

the twig they once held. Come midnight,
you won't see today flipping to tomorrow.

Only the crosshatched shadows of the night
the sun will spend all morning erasing.

American Water

They didn't trust the other country's water,
the crystal ropes uncoiling from the faucets,

so they brought their own in plastic bottles
that vibrated on the cargo plane—cases

mounted on cases mounted on pallets.
In five gallon jugs they brought their own,

shouldered and flipped into a cooler
where the water babbled and released

ghostly balloons whenever a guard was thirsty.
Once it was snow until the sun pummeled it

down the mountain face. As witnessed
only by monumental pines, the water stretched

cellophane across the skulls of boulders.
It drove the fish forward—bug-eyed arrows.

The guards drank their own, but showered
with the country's, mouths clamped

against any bacteria that fell upon their heads.
Some even distrusted the water

that boiled over the burner, the glistening peas,
the nubby, nail-less fingers of carrots.

Some believed the water was good
for one thing: to drench the cloth

pressed against the prisoner's face.
The water seeped into the nostrils,

the burning lungs, until a human voice
sprung from below the hand, saying anything.

Mosul

The donkey. The donkey pulling the cart.
The caravan of dust. The cart made of plywood,
of crossbeam and junkyard tires. The donkey
made of donkey. The long face. The long ears.
The curled lashes. The obsidian eyes blinking
in the dust. The cart rolling, cracking the knuckles
of pebbles. The dust. The blanket over the cart.
The hidden mortar shells. The veins of wires.
The remote device. The red light. The donkey
trotting. The blue sky. The rolling cart. The dust
smudging the blue sky. The silent bell of the sun.
The Humvee. The soldiers. The dust-colored
uniforms. The boy from Montgomery, the boy
from Little Falls. The donkey cart approaching.
The dust. The laughter on their lips. The dust
on their lips. The moment before the moment.
The shockwave. The dust. The dust. The dust.

2

Everything I'm About to Tell You Actually Happened

December. Again the family gathers
around the plastic pine, branches that bend
like pipe cleaners. Sister whitens the tree
with canned snow. Grandma's glass eye
looks more real than her real one.
Father assembles the tree which slept
eleven months in a cardboard box
labeled TREE. Brother tells everyone
the eggnog tastes like arsenic
and fakes his own death. We laugh
our phony laugh and nobody informs him
arsenic is tasteless. Mother wears
a clip-on smile thanks to the tablet
that dissolved beneath her tongue.
Grandpa does that trick with his thumb.
You know, the thumbless hand one.
Doorbell rings. It's Jesus. Drops of blood
fall from his body like a torn bag of rubies.
Together we take him apart and seal him
inside a box labeled MR. KILL JOY.
All night I hear him pounding the cardboard
like distant thunder. Next morning
I ride my new bicycle, crash it full-speed
into an actual tree. Let me tell you
what it's like to be unconscious.
Picture the green field of the world,
a stone well on the perimeter.
Picture a cardboard box at the bottom
of the well. Guess who's inside it.

Self-Portrait with Baby Possum

That's me halfway up the ladder,
crouched beneath the roofline.

That's me gloved. Slanted on the shingles,
that's a paper plate, peanut butter

banged from a spoon. Silence now
except for the wind chime pinging behind me,

the distant screams of schoolchildren
delivered by wind. I'm listening

for the ratatat of claws
and here they come clicking over the roof.

Here comes his pink nose, the rat tail
following his toddling. My hand

in the air, my mind in the air, thinking
Now, wait, now. Such a sound

the animal makes in my grasp,
static in the throat, both hiss

and breath. Down the rungs I climb,
the youngest of three. The fourth

seeped through my mother's fingers
at the foot of the stairs, at the end

of her descending. Such a sound that went
ripping through the house.

The wind chime silently hangs.
No bells in the blue sky. That's me

down from the ladder, holding the possum
up to my face, looking at his looking—

eyes puny, glassed over, rigid
in their sockets, darker than mine.

I Made a Door

Took a plank and sawed it in half, the pieces
small, horizontal, I painted them white,

then drilled the hinges in. Outside the house
I climbed a ladder, up to the fold of roof

over roof, gap to the attic.
I took a hammer. I took the door,

my homespun contraption, one-way
swinging thing, and drove in the nails,

forbade for once raccoons and possums
from entering the darkest of rooms,

but not from leaving. Or so I believed.
Sounds over my head the following week,

paws on wood, the tapping claws, slow rasp
of fur scraping against the air ducts.

Next morning I walked the perimeter
of the house, I turned in right angles,

eyes to the eaves. One thought.
Two. How did he slip in? What other errors

will my muddling hands make?
Failure enters the mind, finds a fissure

and burrows into the marrow of me.
Says I am flawed from head to heels.

Says I am all mistakes down to my cells,
then amends my serotonin.

I was wrong from the start:
The door made me.

At the Post Office

The line is long, processional, glacial,
and the attendant a giant stone, cobalt blue
with flecks of white, I'm not so much
looking at a rock but a slab of night.
The stone asks if anything inside the package
is perishable. When I say no the stone
laughs, muted thunderclap, meaning
everything decays, not just fruit
or cut flowers, but paper, ink, the CD
I burned with music, and my friend
waiting to hear the songs, some little joy
after chemo eroded the tumor. I know flesh
is temporary, and memory a tilting barn
the elements dismantle nail by nail.
I know the stone knows a millennia of rain
and wind will even grind away
his ragged face, and all of this slow erasing
is just a prelude to when the swelling
universe burns out, goes dark, holds
nothing but black holes, the bones of stars
and planets, a vast silence. The stone
is stone-faced. The stone asks how soon
I want the package delivered. As fast
as possible, I say, then start counting the days.

Supermarkets This Large

They bloom and loom in cities no one notices.
High-walled, million-bricked, a roof on cloud turf.

All the letters and numbers are here, all the senses.
Even if you don't need a tub of mayo or Monet

knockoff, it's nice to know you know where to go.
Into the traffic of carts and chattering, a woman

merges with a dozen boxes of Kleenex Softique.
A man in overalls reads out loud his shopping list

as if uttering ceremonial phrases. When one
looks closely at the display cabinets that hold

the glittering watches, one's breath on the glass
is an apparition playing peek-a-boo. I'm flatfooted

in the last row in the furthest aisle. I'm feverish
with colored spots fireworking in my periphery.

I hear someone say, *Here we don't die, we shop.*
I hear someone reply, *Once we stop denying death*

everything tastes better. Meanwhile, a forklift
beeps as it lowers crates of strawberries, hundreds

huddled between the wooden slats. Little hearts.
Hungry tongues. It depends who you believe.

Panoramic

1.

I take a short walk down a long road and come to
a small bird made smaller by a flurry of ants.

I come to a chain-link fence, a grassy field
harassed by October wind. I come to a panorama.

First, my ears take down a hawk, its red shriek
tapering off to silence. Second, my eyes unpin

its stretched wings from a ragged cloud.
Third to seventh isn't worth mentioning,

but eighth is: mourners having a picnic.
It's solemn business eating with a plastic spork

while wearing funeral attire. Round the table
goes the fruit salad, goes the bowl of tears

and hotdog buns. The whole scene gives off
the stillness of a 14th century Dutch painting

until a boom of thunder sends them fleeing
the way a car backfiring makes a line of crows

erupt from a tree limb. Raindrops stipple
the sidewalk as I hurry home to the antidote

of your hands. When the time comes to lie down
beside you, I'll begin forgetting what my eyes

have recorded: the dead bird, a shrieking hawk,
mourners scattering under the flashing sky.

2.

The dead something, a shrieking something,
something scattering under the flashing something.

Obituary

Newspaper tossed from the newspaper boy
was added to the stack, was headlines

resting on yesterday's headlines resting on
the day before's. There were other stacks,

other pillars of newsprint that leaned in a house
swarming with cats. He talked to himself

and his wife who was ash inside an urn,
fine strands of silver woven into a hairbrush.

His hair was steel wool and his yellow nails
claws and the cats moved around the house

with the grace of smoke. The newspapers
leaned the way his body leaned over a cane

with ninety plus years piled atop his shoulders.
Yes he smoked and yes he left a cigarette

lit on the glass ashtray, but no he didn't burn
down the house. But death anyway

in the hallway surrounded by months of crime
astrology sports and three-paneled comics.

Now the afterlife with his wife greeting him
or nothing but nothing as newspapers

continued thumping on his lawn and the cats
curled their tails into question marks.

Kindergarten

We took turns on the wooden stool—
chin up, mouth shut, spine plumb,

frozen. A slide-projector brightened
one side of us, halving the body with light.

My name was called, I took the seat
and stiffened my limbs—boy in amber,

fossilized in front of the class.
The shadow of my head fell over

black construction paper
as Ms. Garcia traced my profile.

Scissors next, whispering in my hand
as I cut along the coastline of my face,

scraps of paper curling to the desk
like the flayed skin of fruit.

Our silhouettes were taped
to windows, our faces floated in sky,

we were twenty-two thunderclouds
holding our rain, twenty-two holes

in cerulean blue. The bell did its bell thing,
our shadows chased us to the grass,

to the sand where Mauricio hung
upside down on the monkey bars,

face dawning with blood. His shirt
peeled down to shoulders, violet clouds

crowded his back. Some looked
like faces. Others, fingerprints.

Snowman

In a coffin his father came back to him,
born from the belly of a cargo plane.
The flag kept the coffin warm, but not his father,
not his arms or lotus-white face.

But not his heart, pomegranate in the fridge.
Meanwhile, snow powders Minnesota
where his son still breathes.
Jacketed with hands buried

in the darkness of mittens, he builds
his father. Snow feet, snow legs
and torso, his head more skull than head,
his eyes cat's eye marbles

he fetched from a drawer where they rolled
and rolled. Out of laziness he left out
his arms, but pennies he pushed
into his chest—medals or shrapnel.

Hornet's Nest

It hung from the eaves like a dome-light
until I knocked it down with a branch
the wind snapped from a sycamore three stories high.
The branch fell, then the nest, then the ants
bustled in and out of the frail structure:
crepe paper walls, pale gray, more air
than anything else. One westward breeze
would've sent it to my neighbor's driveway
where an ambulance rolled up a week ago. Rolled out.
Into the nest the ants came and went, demolishing
the larvae snug inside their hexagonal cells.
Imagine all the mandibles. The ceaseless scissoring.
So too the departed are taken apart and ferried elsewhere.
I washed my hands, poured a bowl of flakes, forgot
until the following day I followed the ants
spooling past the trashcans, underneath the gate,
and there below the window, in the blue
shade of the house where the nest had fallen
upside down on a patch of moss, I saw a skull
crowning through the green world.

Closer

My neighbor kneels
on his lawn,

a chainsaw wailing
in his hands.

The sky turns
a darker lilac, the saw

sings a higher howl
as the spinning chain

cuts a tree stump
leveled across

cinderblocks.
He brings the blocks

closer, halves
the stump again.

Moves the blocks,
halves the halves,

sawdust fountaining
down to the grass.

So a thing that grows
slowly in rings

is diminished in minutes.
So a thing goes

as night charcoals
toward the skyline

and the moon turns
a brighter bone.

3

Man with Swatter

On his front porch, on a folding chair.
A scowl governing his face.

In his left hand, a beer can. The right,
the plastic handle and mesh, spotted

with casualties. Tiny fly guts. Petite
fly wings crumpled like candy wrappers.

The noonday sun hammers his house,
nails its brown shadow to the dirt.

When he lifts his left hand, he's quenched.
The right, another fly's deleted from the world.

Look closely at the ferociousness
of his swing—the way his face, for half

a second, becomes even more deformed,
even more like a jack-o-lantern's—

and you will understand how a man
could kill another man. Without a thought.

One quick move. The air whistling
before his hands lie still as tarantulas.

Victory Song

Soon as we captured the flag we didn't want it anymore.
Soon as nothing flapped on the pole—the sky naked,
the clouds nonexistent. Soon as all that blue
stretched above us, staked to the four corners

of the horizon. Where the wind played tag with itself.
Where gunfire perforated the air and ricocheted
in our minds. Soon as our weapons cooled in our hands.
Soon as the flies arrived, twitching over the flesh

of the soon to be buried, soon to be remembered.
Someone in the battalion began singing the victory song
soon as the lyrics came to him. Then it was sundown
and the multitude of stars made bullet holes

in the night's ceiling. Then our faces glowed tangerine
soon as cigarettes were lit. Soon as we shed our uniforms
we lay down in our cots. We wanted to run
soon as our unlaced boots stood legless in the dark.

Challenging Mud (1955)

after Kazuo Shiraga

Mud as pigment, as mound of burnt sienna,
his body hurled into it. Limbs as brushes

sliding through the sludge, pulling
against his pulling. One's eye

can follow his markings,
swoops in the ooze,

passage of dragging
arms and legs, his struggle

made visible. One's mind can weigh
the cumbersome minutes in the muck.

This one-man scuffle with earth
took place in Tokyo

a decade after Hiroshima, Nagasaki,
those two knotted columns of smoke

growing from the rippling skyline,
the mammoth cloud atop

a brain folding in on itself.
220,000 is too abstract. Think one

farmer, a soybean field,
rows of green to the horizon. Stillness

of his face that morning,
salmon-colored in the salmon sun.

Bootprints in the mist-dampened soil,
a stitched line from home

to shed, shed to field.
Those barely-there impressions.

Doomed (1975)

after Chris Burden

The artist lies beneath a sheet of glass
angled down from the museum wall.
A clock records the minutes that pass.

A crowd huddles as though in biology class
around a cadaver. They watch enthralled
the artist lying beneath a sheet of glass.

Some applaud and whistle. Others harass.
Two men debate *What is art?* until they brawl.
The clock records the minutes that pass.

Ten hours lapse when sunlight tips the grass,
but in the museum nothing had changed at all:
the artist is still beneath the sheet of glass.

No one there imagines he will last
another evening on the floor. Time stalls
while the clock records the minutes that pass.

America is still in the morass
of Vietnam, but in two weeks Saigon will fall.
An artist lies beneath a sheet of glass.
A clock records the minutes that pass.

Retirement Home Melee at the Salad Bar

They say it began with an elderly man
foraging through the icebergs and romaines.

They say another who prefers his salad
without a stranger's fingerprints

said *Stop*. From there, they say, curses
hissed through dentures. From there, fists.

They say it was a fracas, knocked bifocals
and clattering canes, the wooden screech

of chair legs, some to break up the scuffle
and some to shuffle off on a bad knee,

or pinned hip, or pace-makered heart.
One is bitten, they say. Another wears

a cut across his forehead, blood flowing
down the canals of his wrinkles.

Next day's the same old same old,
as they say. Back to the quiet swing

of living without velocity or fire.
Shuffleboard and Pinochle, the dull

click of knitting needles, their final
gray years going limp. Or so they say.

The Body You're Suited-up In

The night peels the sun like an orange,
swallows it wedge by wedge. Come dawn,
the sun will rise again for you, bronze

and blazing. You take this for granted,
and this and this and this. There were days
when *seize the day* worked, when uttering

the phrase was an epiphany mint
sweetening your tongue. Now you might
as well be saying *seize the hammock.*

And the skull you keep on a cluttered desk
wearing a toupee of dust, how it functions
more as a paperweight than a reminder

the body you're suited-up in is a body
death is slowly unzipping. What you need
is another slogan, another *memento mori*

to replace that skull. May I suggest
an X-ray of your chest Scotch-taped
to the kitchen window, that every morning

you study closely your heart, caught
like a child's balloon in the branches of ribs.
Ghost-pale, as if turning to dust. Which it will.

Phantom Limb

A train devouring wind and a woman
on the tracks, too much wine, too little
wisdom, the moon powdering her skin

the blue of apparitions. One second
later, one less limb. One week later,
crutches give a pulse to her apartment,

a low thumping her neighbor below drinks
with lifted ears until his head is woozy
with her movement. Hellos in the hall,

hellos in the hum of clothes fumbling
in the laundry room. Finally his hands
find the crimson wounds of geraniums

wrapped in cellophane, his knuckles rouse
the heartbeat sleeping inside her door.
She opens the door. She opens the door

of her mouth and says, *Come in, come in.*
After a season of hands and lips
she gives his eyes her missing leg, flesh

from thigh to knee, bedsheet from knee
to foot. To her mouth he presses his mouth.
To her body, his body. Three legs

braiding, unbraiding, and the wind
of their breath, the wind of the night
brushing the dark X-ray of the window.

Married And

Married and the door to her office
locked from the inside, a wooden door
with faces spiraled in the grain.

And a Sunday, and our hands,
our mouths, our hands and tongues,
an air-conditioner's low hum,

the strip of tissue tied to the vent
squiggling its red line. And our tongues.
Married and her son's 5x7 on her desk,

aluminum bat propped and sun-dazzled
on his shoulder, eyes blindfolded
by the cap's shadow. Her blouse

flayed open, my hands, her lavender bra,
my hands. Married and her husband
somewhere over the Mediterranean,

eyes reading or shut, the oval windows
of the plane tinted with evening.
Down below, the dark water,

rise and dip of bottlenose dolphins,
the frequency of their clicks
disrupting the sonar.

Hangover

A knife in the mind, a desert

in the throat. Kaleidoscope
of bottles in the trash.

Slowly is the only way

I can move into the yard,
the morning gauzed in mist.

On the lawn, a paper plate

dotted with cake crumbs,
a flurry of ants. I think

through the throbbing

and the night spools back
in scraps, the gaps in-between

large, deleted for good.

A little like death. Or nowhere
near. What dying will do

with memories I can only

speculate: crumbs
left on a plate or carried

one and one into the grass.

Housefly

It's all zip and right angles, tracing
a square in space above the glass
coffee table. Just red mosaic eyes
and furred body, cellophane wings
beating 300 times per second. Never
mind I'm all right angles too—work,
market, bank, home; work, market,
bank, home—the pest needs to go.
And by go I mean this yellow swatter,
the snap of my wrist. I mean this fly
now wriggling on the floor, a period
searching for the end of a sentence.

4

The Pompous Man

Blowhard. Windbag. Bagpipe
bemoaning my eardrums.
Dictionary tongue, unabridged,
ruffling its pages. Vocabulary
vaunter ladling the Latin, a pinch
of French. Stuck up. Stick up
the you-know-what. *The bum,*
he would say. *The derrière.*
So hoity-toity. High and mighty.
Walking library. White hair
combed Roman column straight.
Know-it-all. Read-it-all.
Wrote-it-and-published-it-all.
Firework show of intellect
blossoming across the brain.
Spectacle in spectacles. Mind
on the loose in the labyrinth,
mouth hitched like a caboose.
Anecdote, opinion, anecdote,
pun. He quits when he lifts
liqueur to his lips, letting go
what he holds most dear: our ears.

[handwritten annotations in margins: "allusion to a favorite poem", "alcohol or chemical related", "speaking from the thing", "vs. chemical induction"]

Mosh

My knees are her knees
are his knees.
Same goes with elbows.

We shove collectively
where the wave
says to shove, knowing

it will roll back to us
more furious.
Heat from our bodies

rises eye-level,
our shirts sodden
and holding skin

like leaves to sidewalk
after a downpour.
How lovely the one

crushed beside me,
her slippery arm
flush against mine.

When spotlights
burn yellow, so do we.
Blue, ditto.

Now she's towed
to the outermost ring
by circumstance

as strobes of white
turn the whirling
mob off and on—

a wheat field
windblown beneath
blasts of lightning.

Against Erosion

Certain is the surgeon in his surgical gown
as the scalpel enters the swabbed flesh
of the woman in the surgical light.
How intimate is all the pulling, fingers
massaging her face, the slackening
skin tucked like a bed sheet.
Two days before stitches are clipped,
railroading around her crown.
Gone a decade into the curls of hair,
the dread of cameras and mirrors.

A woman makes certain strides
past the sliding gaze of certain men,
their whistles and sighs and double-
takes, but soon winter goes, spring
resurrects green. Swiftly the seasons
undress, months peel from the wall,
and newer wrinkles crease the flesh.
Gone the comfortable lead ahead of time,
the sprightly bounce in her footsteps

before a pen glides along her face again.
Anesthesia brings a dream of waves
destroying a shore. A safeguard tower
kneels to the water, beach umbrellas
swept and pinwheeling. Gone the slabs
of cliff, the cypress trees, guardrail
and road. Gone the surrendering earth
into the colossal blue where it was born.

Head Case

The biologist who carried the severed
head of a harbor seal to the airport

was without a permit to carry
such a thing. To carry such a thing

his head was somewhere else
besides the mantel of his shoulders.

Elsewhere is where his head was
like the head of the seal he carried,

a mammal that once spiraled below
the waves like a thought wandering.

Detained and questioned, nodding
to authorities like an ocean buoy.

The biologist's head must've been
somewhere else. Hovering over

a microscope or underneath
a showerhead. Three days without

Paxil and my own head ends up
blowing bubbles on the bottom

of depression's pool. My head then
is still my head but one I'd trade

any day for the seal's lustrous
and whiskered one. Medicated,

I can tolerate it perched on my neck
like now as the ocean booms and sighs

beside me, and further out the sun lays
its golden head on the horizon's guillotine.

Velvet

1.

The downsliding mind of a man holding
a kitchen knife and tin bucket.

In the bathroom light, one glints
while one reflects the wallpaper
around its cylinder, flowers stretching
all the way to the brim.

The progression of thought
can only be imagined: *I will
end myself without making a mess.*

A handyman, he needed only
two tools: knife, bucket.
One to let out the blood. One to hold it.

2.

But the body has a mind of its own.
It wants to go on, go on.

His wife finds him in the living room,
waxen, gills on the wrists.
The night rolls this into memory,

and this: quick medics,
the clattering stretcher and swiveling

siren, curbside birch tree
with its arterial branches
pulsing in the ambulance-light.

3.

For months I held him in my mind.
Correction: what he did
held onto me.

Above my bed the bucket swayed,
the blade was angled
so I could see myself.

People would ask me
how I was doing and I would say *good*.
One season into the next,

from December's cold logic
to the bare branches of mid-March
now clicking outside my window.

No, not bare:
velvet, wine-colored leaves
sprouting from the joints.

On Aggression

My beautiful, bowlegged, jade-eyed tabby
was lounging on the patio
when a sparrow, swooping
down from the blue,

thumped against the screen door. And there
it thrashed, its claws
caught in the mesh.
How swiftly this all happened

from where I sat on the living room couch
reading about the war—
the cat darted, leapt, his outstretched body
rising and rising

until the sparrow fluttered
in his jaws. No time to think—
the newspaper skated
across the wooden floor,

the door screeched along its track,
my hands clamped around the cat's throat
and squeezed, blood shuttling
quicker through my veins.

Drop it, I commanded,
and he obeyed. I let go. The sparrow
scuttled on the concrete
before ruffling a line in the lawn,

then sailed over the trellis
mobbed with lavender flowers,
over a rooftop, the black arrow
of its shadow sliding across the shingles.

The world slowed then, the blood cooled.
Far off, wind jostled wind chimes—
the sound of a broom
endlessly sweeping broken glass.

Fear and Logic

Citizens, we were hoodwinked.
They played our hearts

like funeral bagpipes so doom
was in our blood, so death

was the shadow of tomorrow
that charcoaled the office party,

the family picnic. We were
spooked, Citizens. Our evening's

soundtrack was the first black key
pressed on the piano, thunder

hammered from a wire.
Any minute a phosphorescent

window and the ceiling
on our backs, our bodies

dusted with drywall. But then
we were dreaming, Citizens—

if the sun yo-yoed beyond
the green hills, if a river

flowed backwards and up
a waterfall, if a beheaded

magician pulled his own head
out of a hat, it made sense

as it always will to our eyes
when they are closed.

Road Trip

A car detonates and your television flattens
the aftermath, a car that is not a car anymore
but the mouth of a crater. Bodies too, bodies
once upright with breath in their mouths.
A car detonates on Tuesday, on Wednesday,
two days later a car detonates and bodies
flattened under concrete, blood marbling
the road. Spring to summer and cars to not-cars,
breaths to not-breaths, to blood in the mouths.
Car on the road and you behind the wheel,
a song in your mouth. The song is green
and goes out the window where the horizon
is flattened. Your car goes and the song
goes and summer crushes down its heat,
sun on your windshield and the constellation
of insects flattened by speed. No television
or news reels. Just song and highways,
just landscape. A hawk in the dusk-light
hovering seven stories above the crimson earth.

The Big Nothing, or the Gap Between David Letterman's Teeth

Through a tunnel goes my mind: if
the universe is a giant balloon
expanding, what's on the other side
of the latex, what's around
the porcelain rim if the universe
is a dinner plate, and if a book
is the universe, what's outside
the bound cover, what's beyond
the words? If nil, if zero, zilch,

zip, how did the void appear,
how did it unfold the black cloth
of nothing? Through a hole
goes this thought and soon
I've made a balloon of my heart,
rising toward the night sky
and its needle-pointed stars.
Anxiety again and no Xanax
while my wife sleeps in the bedroom,
while I flicker on the couch
watching the glowing window
of the television, while my mind
goes and goes: for any object
to exist, space for that object
must exist. As when a sparrow
darts across the sky, the sky
fills where the sparrow's been.
Through a tunnel, through a hole:
God is the Big Nothing that allows
you to move around in this world,

sparrows to thread the air,
and the late-night talk show host
to pitch a blue card through
an imaginary window, wherein
someone plays a recording of glass
breaking, wherein I lift the remote
and surround myself with a silence
that was there from the beginning.

NOTES

"Questions About Butterflies" was inspired by Damien Hirst's exhibit "Superstition" at the Gagosian Gallery in Beverly Hills.

"Proof" is for Adam Karsten.

"At the Post Office" is for Brian Padian.

In "Panoramic," the phrases "First, my ears take down a hawk" and "It's solemn business eating with a plastic spork" are reconfigurations of two lines by Charles Simic, one from his poem "Dismantling the Silence" ("Take down its ears first . . .") and the other from "To All Hog-Raisers, My Ancestors" ("When I eat pork, it's solemn business").

Ernie Liang

DAVID HERNANDEZ's poetry collections include *Always Danger* (Southern Illinois University Press, 2006), winner of the Crab Orchard Series in Poetry, and *A House Waiting for Music* (Tupelo Press, 2003). A recipient of a NEA fellowship, Hernandez's poems have appeared in *Field, Ploughshares, The Threepenny Review, The Missouri Review, AGNI* and *The Southern Review*. He is also the author of two YA novels, *No More Us for You* and *Suckerpunch*, both published by HarperTeen. David lives in Long Beach and is married to writer Lisa Glatt. Visit his website at www.DavidAHernandez.com.